Joe Dannis is owner of DawnSignPress, and Executive Producer of DawnPictures. Joe graduated in 1978 from Gallaudet, the university for deaf people, where he first met co-author Ben Bahan. Joe has been a leader in the field of production and publication of educational sign language and deaf culture materials. Under Joe's direction, DawnSignPress has provided the means for pulling together critical information to acknowledge and meet the growing demand for sign language education.

Ben Bahan, a graduate of Gallaudet University, is well known for his expertise in language acquisition, bilingualism and American Sign Language. He received his M.A. from Boston University, where he is currently the director of the undergraduate program in Deaf Studies. His unequaled contributions come from his long experience as an author of numerous books including the most popular *Signs For Me*. Ben and Joe have combined their talents in both publishing and the critical blending of ASL with English to bring this book to you.

Patricia Pearson is a classically-trained graphic artist and illustrator who received her art education at Art Center in Pasadena and the Academy of Arts in San Francisco. Formerly an advertising illustrator, she has here fulfilled a long-time desire to illustrate children's books.

MY ABC SIGNS OF ANIMAL FRIENDS
Authors: BEN BAHAN, JOE DANNIS
Illustrator: PATRICIA PEARSON

© 1994 by DawnSignPress. All rights reserved.
Published 1994. Printed in korea

10 9 8 7 6 5 4

ISBN 0-915035-31-6

MY ABC SIGNS OF ANIMAL FRIENDS

BEN BAHAN & JOE DANNIS
ILLUSTRATED BY PATRICIA PEARSON

DawnSignPress
San Diego, California

INTRODUCTION

You and the children are about to begin a wonderful journey into the world of signing. Here you will discover the very foundations for American Sign Language (ASL)–demonstrated as never before by 26 friends from the animal kingdom! From Alec the Alligator to Zach the Zebra, they all team up to help you help the children learn their ABCs.

American Sign Language began as the language of deaf people, but is becoming evermore popular with hearing people. That is why this book was published. It is meant for both hearing and deaf adults who know the importance and ease of teaching languages to children at a time when young minds are most receptive.

Now, the rest is up to you. Teach the children, and learn along with them as our gentle animal friends step you through each letter of the English alphabet.

HOW TO SIGN THE ANIMALS

First look at the building blocks containing the alphabet. They show the handshape that corresponds to each letter of the English alphabet. Then notice that some of the words are fingerspelled, where you spell out each individual letter.

Next, notice the red arrows beside the hands in most of the signs. The arrows point *in the direction* the sign is to be made.

Other arrows show you the *path* of the direction in which to sign.

The zig-zagged arrows mean you need to *repeat* a movement twice or more. You sign in the direction of the arrow and then return to do it quickly once again.

Signs without arrows have short little lines around them to show that you'll use a *wiggling* motion to sign.

Okay now, is everybody ready? It's time for your exciting journey. We wish you the fullest success and the richest rewards as you expand the minds of children in this special dimension of communication that can serve them, and you, for a lifetime.

Alec the alligator.

Betty the bird.

Conrad the cat.

Derek the duck.

Elly the elephant.

Fanny the fish.

George the giraffe.

Ho the hippopotamus.

Irene the iguana.

Jill the jackrabbit.

Kelly the kangaroo.

Leroy the lion.

Megan the mouse.

Nina the newt.

Ollie the octopus.

Pedro the pig.

Quincy the quail.

Robert the raccoon.

Sarah the squirrel.

Theo the turtle.

Ursula the unicorn.

Valerie the vulture.

Willie the worm.

Xaveria the fox.

Yutaka the yak.

Zach the zebra.